A Precious LOSS

Beyond the Pain of Miscarriage and Infant Death

A Precious LOSS

Beyond the Pain of Miscarriage and Infant Death

Sharon Fox

Published by Redemption Press, PO Box 427, Enumclaw, WA 98022
Toll Free (844) 2REDEEM (273-3336)

Redemption Press is honored to present this title in partnership with the author. The views expressed or implied in this work are those of the author. Redemption Press provides our imprint seal representing design excellence, creative content and high quality production.

ISBN 13: 978-1-68314-033-7 (Print)
         978-1-68314-035-1 (ePub)
         978-1-68314-036-8 (Mobi)

Library of Congress Catalog Card Number: 2016941559

A Precious Loss was written to offer to those who have experienced a miscarriage, Sudden Infant Death Syndrome (SIDS)/infant death, or stillborn a window into the grief process. It presents the biblical grief model and the emotions to expect after a loss, and it includes the steps to move toward contentment. My thanks to LifeTalk Pregnancy Center in Frisco, Texas, for identifying the need for Christian-based material specifically addressing the loss of a baby due to miscarriage.

It is my prayer that as you read the material you will experience a healing of your wounded soul and find the Holy Spirit, your divine Comforter, at work in your life.

Illustrations by Katie Arani

Contents

Acknowledgments ix
How to Use this Book xi

Chapter 1—What to Expect. 1
Chapter 2—Your Wounded Soul 6
Chapter 3—God's Model of Grieving 10
Chapter 4—What Do You Do Now? 15
Chapter 5—Where Is Hope? 34
Chapter 6—How Do You Find Happy? 41
Chapter 7—Intimacy after Miscarriage, SIDS/Infant Death, or Stillbirth. 44
Chapter 8—What Should *You* Say to Someone Who Is Grieving? 48
Chapter 9—Holding on to Hope. 50
Chapter 10—The Bed 52

About the Author, About Brave Penny Nonprofit. 57

Acknowledgments

A HUGE THANK YOU to those who supported me by patiently reading and correcting the text: my sisters, Marilyn Muecke and Carolyn Pittenger, Brave Penny Board members, Paul Jones, H. B. Bartz, friends Deborah Phillips, Toni Salmon, Diane Sanderson and Mistie Coblentz of Life Talk. I also want to thank the other Brave Penny Board members: Denise Price, Patricia Prior (who encouraged me to include the material on SIDS and Infant death), and Heather Finney Rodrigues for their faithful prayers during the writing process. Many thanks go to the "Weaver Sisters": Rev. Toni Brown, Debbie Finn, Gail Bernard, Ginny Lydick, and Patty Woodmansee for walking with me over the years as sisters in Christ.

There are not words to adequately say Thank You to my husband, Jim, who has patiently and generously supported me as I write in obedience to God's call to serve those who grief. You made this book possible. I love you for loving me. I thank God every day for you. To God be the Glory!

How to Use this Book

MOST OF THE materials in this book are for all readers who have experienced grief of any kind. The book addresses the concepts of the Wounded Soul and God's Model for Grieving, which have universal application to all types of losses. These two concepts explain the recovery path from a profound loss. Losses would include death of a parent, spouse, adult child or the loss related to a divorce, job, pet and/or health, which carry deep feelings of bereavement. Losses from experiencing a miscarriage, SIDS death, Infant death, or stillborn death are separated from other types of loss because of an additional loss element. The death of a child is also the loss of the dream for that child's life. All loving parents hold a hope for their child to experience love, joy, and success in what would have been a normal life span. When a baby dies, so dies the dream.

Where appropriate, there are notations of specific loss types to aid in ease of reading. This book is easily adaptable to a reader who is anxious for the highlights that make the book quickly impactful. Skip the parts that don't apply to you, like Name the Baby if your child died of SIDS/Infant death or was stillborn. Let me take the bold step to suggest that the reader who wants to get to the bottom line on grief recovery read the following sections first:

Chapter 2 – Your Wounded Soul
Chapter 3 – God's Model of Grieving
Finding Hope in the Christian Faith on page 7
Empty Arms on page 20
Shadow Grief on page 21
Plan to Be Content Again on page 35
Chapter 10 – The Bed

Blessings as you read and learn about grief.

CHAPTER 1

What to Expect

What Should a Mother and Father Expect when Grieving the Loss of their Child?

Your path of grief will be unique. Your spouse and other family or friends who are closely involved will have a totally different experience. Neither your reaction and feelings nor theirs are right or wrong. They are different. It is important to remember that men and women grieve differently. Society and culture form the grief response for both males and females by giving or withholding permission for emotional responses. Be careful not to hold on to expectations for your spouse's behavior. His or her response will likely not be on the same path of time and emotion as yours. God designed you to be unique so you are different from any other human and your grief journey will be a unique experience, not to be measured against the reactions of others.

Mother's Loss

For the mother, the emotional assault that is combined with the physical impact of the pregnancy or miscarriage or coping with a seriously sick child creates stress that does not lend itself to words. What do you do now? Where do you go from this dark emotional place? How do you cope in silence? Do you talk about this? How do you talk about this?

Jumbled responses and concern slam into reality. Sadness and confusion are the dense air that surrounds a miscarriage or an infant death.

Loss for the mother is a very intimate and personal experience. Often even close friends and family are not there to support or express care because (in the case of a miscarriage) the event has occurred so early in the pregnancy. When SIDS, infant death, or stillbirth has occurred, family and friends are also grieving. They may be unable to care for the parents when support is needed the most. Through the miracle of conception, the joining of two cells has formed a baby. There is an expectation of a baby, child, and adolescent and then adulthood as the natural sequence of life order. When that order is disrupted, the loss causes the mother to suffer on several levels.

First, the physical loss of the baby may create a need for surgical intervention to resolve the aftermath of the miscarriage. The recovery from surgery and the interruption of work or daily routines are suddenly an unavoidable reality. Clarity of thinking and ability to follow up on normal tasks become bewildering and debilitating.

Next, if there are other children in the home, they will sense that things are somehow not normal. Children may react to the changes in routine by displaying sadness or acting out. Even if they don't know about the miscarriage and what that means, they are now aware that their mother is not happy. If they had known of and were anticipating a new sibling and a stillbirth has occurred, they will also grieve the loss of a happy parent or parents. If they have been a sibling of a child who dies of SIDS or an infant death, the death is real and should be addressed with care and love.

Finally, the loss of the dreams for the child's life add to the suffering of the parents. The emotional impact of disappointment is often a burden so intense that the need to recoil from life activities and interactions is intense.

Mothers are subject to a normal reaction that may exclude others from their communication circle. Husbands, children, family, and friends can find themselves "exiled" not by intention, but from the experience of loss, which leaves the mother without energy or optimism to apply to other relationships.

It is critical that special attention is paid to communicating in an honest way with the father, with other children, and the extended family. The mother's emotional isolation can damage her and her family relationships if not carefully tended. Mothers should make sure to use what little energy they have to keep the communication lines open.

Grandparents should be included in the circle of loss as well. Their loss may include the sadness they feel not only for themselves, but the witness of the sadness of their son or daughter and spouse who are so wounded by this loss. Grandparents grieve as deeply as the parents in some cases, as they are seeing generational loss that is powerful and personal.

Father's Loss

For the father who has been actively involved in the pregnancy and/or life of the child, the feelings of disappointment and heartfelt sadness will be new and possibly so unexpected that he can hardly function. Not only is he experiencing the loss of the baby but also the recognition that the baby's mother is physically and emotionally struggling. This dual concern often creates for him an additional sense of helplessness and frustration. That combination of unexpected circumstances and emotions can lead to relationship difficulties between the parents. Careful attention to the relationship post-miscarriage or post-death are important for both the mother and father. It is important for both parents to be patient with one another, as there are no rule books or timetables that apply to the grief process.

A father often finds himself in a "role reversal" situation that is foreign to the normal relationship with his wife. Women are typically the family caretakers. They are the managers of the laundry, meal preparation, and if there are other children in the family, those tasks may include scheduling car pool and sport commitments.

When a miscarriage or death of a baby occurs, those duties fall to the father, who is also grieving. He will need to recognize that his wife is unable to carry on those types of activities for a while as she recovers. He may feel he is ill prepared to assume those tasks. More important than the assumption of tasks is the recognition that when he asks his wife what she wants for dinner, for example, she may be unable to think clearly enough to tell him what she would like to eat. His shock, grief, and loss—rather than neglect of his wife—can hinder his insight to be able to understand that a decision as simple as "soup or a sandwich" can become an insurmountable thought process for her.

It is vitally important to know that when the stress of a miscarriage or infant death occurs, the brain actually does not work the way it should or has worked before. Both parents are impaired for a time. It is important for both mother and father to have realistic expectations of one other. During this grief-laden time, what was normal and easy becomes difficult and dynamically complex. Patience and grace toward one other are critical during the early days and weeks after the loss of a child.

After a Miscarriage

For the mother and father who have experienced a miscarriage, the emotional assault encompasses their entire being. The loss is rarely discussed beyond the immediate circle of family and friends due to the intimacy of the event. Miscarriage brings with it profound sadness, questions about the cause of the miscarriage, and feelings of brokenness. The broken dreams, broken heart, a broken body (for the mother), and wounded souls of the parents are all too often suffered in silence.

The Heartbreak of Sudden Infant Death Syndrome (SIDS)

SIDS is a devastating and mysterious death occurrence in infants. Up to the age of one (three years old is also included in some statistical reports of SIDS), a sudden death can occur and be labeled as a syndrome death. There are many theories about cause and prevention. Your healthcare professional may have shared the current thinking on the topic with you.

For some parents, knowing is important; but knowing changes nothing. A baby has died. The loss is sudden and intimate. Those two elements make the impact of the loss a very precious loss.

In fact, you may never know or be satisfied with the information you learn in research or hear from a professional. The reality is that your baby's body stopped functioning as it should. His or her tiny body made up of many parts (heart, brain, lungs, liver, kidneys, and other organs, as well as air passages, blood vessels, and skeletal frame) failed to work in concert to sustain life. There are many things in life we just don't understand. SIDS is one of those things for many families.

Whatever the cause of the death of your child or how it occurred, research indicates that there are two reactions typically experienced by the parents and/or family members. One is a crisis of faith; the second is a deepening of faith. Read about your wounded soul and map your progress in God's model of grieving that you'll find later in this book. You can find yourself content and actually happy again.

Terminology and Statistics

Illness or Congenital Abnormality

Deaths from illness or congenital abnormalities are different from the more bewildering types of infant deaths as in SIDS and stillbirth. The cause is often known. Infections or heart, lung, or kidney abnormalities take the lives of babies within hours, days, or months and create yet another type of precious loss. These deaths are so unfair and so confusing to the parents when the cause seems to render the family questioning the origins of the life-taking illness or body abnormality. Hope for sustainable life is always a desire, yet in many cases the reality of survival is clearly not possible. Infant death due to illness, genetic abnormalities, or post-birth complications will also be grouped with the SIDS topics.

Infant Death

The death of a child who was alive at birth but died soon after is under the general category of infant death.

Miscarriage

Miscarriage, also known as spontaneous abortion and pregnancy loss, is the natural death of an embryo or fetus before it is able to survive independently. It is also the term used when a pregnancy is not viable, including ectopic pregnancies where medical intervention is required for termination of the pregnancy. Research reports that 25 percent of pregnancies end in miscarriage. (This staggering statistic, especially if you are in that 25 percent group, is so much more than a number to the mother, father, and family of the baby who has not survived. This type of loss is virtually a silent wound to the soul.)

Stillborn–Death at or Prior to Birth

The shock of death instead of the expected live birth is one with horrific impact whether it occurred as an early- or late-term death. Perhaps there was an indication prior to delivery that the baby was no longer alive; or perhaps it was the delivery process that took the life of the baby. The harsh reality of a stillbirth pierces the souls of the parents.

Names had been selected, announcements made ready, nursery assembled, and showers of gifts had been received, all of which now turn to empty hopes and profound loss. Your precious one is lost to you.

Stillbirth refers to the death of a baby in the womb after twenty weeks. Prior to twenty weeks the term is miscarriage. Early stillbirth occurs in the twenty- to twenty-seven-week period; late stillbirth occurs in the twenty-eight to thirty-six-week period; and term stillborn or a stillbirth occurs at or after the thirty-seven-week period. One percent of the births in the United States, or approximately 24,000 births annually are stillbirths. Stillbirths occur ten times more often than SIDS deaths. The exact cause of death is often undetermined, even when medical examination occurs.

SIDS (Sudden Infant Death Syndrome) and SUID (Sudden Unexplained Infant Death)

SIDS is one part of a composite term of infant deaths that occur between birth and one year of age. The term SUID includes all three types of death: SIDS (45 percent), unknown causes of death (31 percent) and accidental suffocation or strangulation (24 percent). Approximately 3,500 SUIDs occurred in 2013 in the United States. SIDS will be used as a universal term in this book for the death of an infant up to one year of age, regardless of the classification listed above.

CHAPTER 2

Your Wounded Soul

PERHAPS IF WE could imagine a physical description of the soul, it might be much like the human heart. It might have a rounded shape, a smooth surface, and substance like a muscle. The soul has been described as the residence of the essence of the human spirit. The soul is the spiritual part of humans, which holds recognition of God, joy, zest for life, contentment, and so much more.

One day the smooth surface of the soul is injured due to a significant loss. When a parent dies, the soul's wound may be a long gash that exposes the innermost part of the organ. In the case of the loss of a parent, there would be a funeral or memorial service with an announcement among friends, which would make the death publicly acknowledged. The wounded soul would be easily "visible" to others and there would be an expected social expression by others of their condolences for the death. Such wounds take time, and are given time, to heal due to the severity of the loss.

A miscarriage is more like a puncture wound into the soul. It has a tiny entry point but the wound goes deep. The outside world would hardly notice the miscarriage wound. When a miscarriage occurs, there is little or no public acknowledgment of the loss. For the parents of a miscarried baby, this wound is profoundly painful and slow to heal. The expected caring and support of others is unavailable or absent due to the silence of the loss.

SIDS, infant death, or stillbirth create a gash on the soul. The shock of the death creates a very deep wound and seems to be visible to others. Unlike the miscarriage wound, which has a tiny entry at death, a child who dies at birth or within the year of birth creates a painful slash that feels almost life-threatening to the parents. How can they survive this horrific assault on their souls?

The old saying, "Time heals all wounds," is a poor description of the reality of loss and recovery. Recovery from loss requires far more than pages on a calendar. When ignored or when an "I'm okay" bandage is applied, the wound is still there. It may appear to blend into the surface, but the deeper part of the wound still exists.

What does the wound on your soul after losing a baby look like? Coming to terms with the wound by imaging its depth and length will help you understand the feelings and behaviors you are experiencing.

Before we move to the more concrete steps of healing, another concept of Christian grief recovery is important to learn.

Finding Hope in the Christian Faith

If you are a Christian, you are likely familiar with the first four books of the New Testament: Matthew, Mark, Luke, and John. They tell of the life and crucifixion (death) of God's Son, Jesus. God mourned the death of his crucified Son in the same pattern or way that we mourn the deaths of our loved ones.

Christians believe in a triune God, meaning Father, Son (Jesus), and Holy Spirit, who are all unified. Triune, which means "three as one," can be a hard concept to grasp if this is your first encounter with Christian faith. Perhaps a brief description of how that works would be helpful before we address the death of Jesus and the pattern of grief.

Three in one can be described with this example: You have three plates before you, each holding a component of an apple. One plate has the peel, one has the pulp, and one has the core with seeds. If you were asked the question "Which one of these is an apple?" how would you respond? Actually, you could not reply that it is just the peel or just the pulp or just the core. They are all "apple." The skin holds the pulp under a safe layer; the pulp encases the core and seeds; while the skin emerges from the ends of the core to cover the pulp. All are a part of the whole, but each is unique as a component. That is how God works. He is both all and the parts of the same divine being as Father, Son, and Holy Spirit.

Another example of the triune God is my favorite explanation. Let's think about a man, and let's name him John. John is the son of Elizabeth, the husband of Ruth, and father of Jacob. Same man but he lives and serves in unique roles. That again is how the Trinity works. God, Jesus, and the Holy Spirit are one, yet they are uniquely individual to us.

In John 1:1-5 we read, "In the beginning was the Word, [meaning Jesus] and the Word was with God, and the Word was God. He was with God in the beginning. Through him all things were made; without him nothing was made that has been made. In him was life, and that life was the light of all mankind. The light shines in the darkness, and the darkness has not overcome it."

Jesus, after taking human form and living a life on earth, said many times in the Bible that he and God were one, including in John 10:30, "I and the Father [God] are one."

God's love for us was so deep that he allowed his Son to die for the sins of all humanity. Jesus lived a perfect, sinless life. But he served as a sacrifice to save or redeem us so that we could live with God through eternity. God mourned the human death of his Son. He understands how grief feels. After Jesus rose from the dead and ascended into heaven forty days later, the Holy Spirit, the third being of the triune God, who had been joined to Jesus at his baptism, was then sent by Jesus to be a Spirit of comfort and a guide for our lives. All three beings integrated into what is called the Holy Trinity. One God of three parts.

We read in Matthew 3:16, "As soon as Jesus was baptized, he went up out of the water. At that moment heaven was opened, and he saw the Spirit of God descending like a dove and alighting on him."

A God who loved humanity so much that he gave his Son as a sacrifice to pay for the sins of the world is not a mean and vindictive God. He is a God who overflows with unconditional love. He does not keep score. He does not remember your sins once you have confessed them. He desires a relationship with us that is based on our trust in him and his gentle love for us. He eagerly awaits your commitment to live in the freedom of his love every day.

God did not cause your child to die. We live in a world that is full of sickness and the fragility of man. The death of your child is not God's fault. The redemption that comes from the love of God for each human allows him to be glorified. It is out of terrible sorrow, tragic loss, and "woundedness" in our lives that restoration and joy can grow into contentment. Somehow, something good can come from this loss if you allow God to love you through the grief. It is a divine mystery that has been proven over and over again through the generations.

CHAPTER 3

God's Model of Grieving

GOD'S MODEL OF grieving is taken from the three days which Christians observe as Easter weekend. It is the pattern of the feeling and journey that God experienced when his child Jesus died. It applies to all types of loss. God's model of the grief journey is a presentation to parents of what to expect as recovery occurs.

Let's begin with what happened on that Friday afternoon, the day that Jesus died. In the book of Matthew, chapter 27, verses 45 and 51, we learn that when Jesus died, there was darkness over the land, and a curtain was torn into two pieces in the temple where the Jews worshiped, and the earth shook:

"From noon until three in the afternoon darkness came over all the land" (Matt. 27:45).

"At that moment the curtain of the temple was torn in two from the top to the bottom. The earth shook, the rocks split. . . ." (Matt. 27:51).

Darkness

The first description is darkness. This darkness is the term used by many to describe the feeling of grief and mourning. It is the profound sadness or the dark period after the loss that has been experienced. The darkness feels like it actually limits the ability to see the future. The cloud of despair wraps itself around you and almost stops you in your tracks. The darkness causes you to feel disoriented, something like a snow storm where you can't see anything and you walk in circles or fall into knee-deep snow. But this white out is close to a total blackout. This is not an endless pit, although it may feel like it is. The darkness will pass. It takes time. As it passes, remember it is a normal reaction to grief.

Tearing of the Fabric of Life

The next piece of the model is the tearing of the curtain in the temple. For you, that would mean the tearing of the fabric of your life. The Jews worshiped in a huge and holy temple during the time of Jesus' life. In the temple, there were several areas designated for specific uses: a public area, a worship area, and a sacred place. A curtain hung between the worship area and the sacred space.

The curtain in the temple was four inches thick and sixty feet tall. Only a force beyond our comprehension could have ripped that curtain from the top to bottom. You may feel the full impact of such a tear in the fabric of your life as you recognize that the daily rhythm and expectations you held are no longer connected; you are no longer on a seamless journey in life.

A thread that has been intertwined or woven into your lives is severed when an adult you love dies. In the case of a miscarriage, a tiny colorful thread that was to be intertwined into the fabric of your life has been abruptly snipped. That thread, with its particular color that was unique to your child, is now severed and will never be seen again in this lifetime. With the absence of the thread, at the abrupt end of the thread is where the pain explodes into your life.

It is important to understand that it is not only that the thread was snipped but where the thread ended there seems to have formed a hole in the fabric of life. The hole demands attention in order to heal. It demands an attempt to stabilize the fabric of life in order to hold the remainder of the fabric together. Like the work of a seamstress, tiny stitches need to circle the hole to insure that the fabric will not unravel. The hole in the fabric of your life, if unattended will cause instability in the remainder of your life. Those tiny stiches are called "grief work." Time and grief work will together repair the hole. The hole in your life will always be there. But it does not need to be, nor should it be the centerpiece of your life. God calls us to live abundantly. Grieve for a time because we are forever changed by this event. You can make the choice to live in contentment so that grief does not take over your future.

Earthquake and Rocks Split

The third aspect of God's model is the earthquake (see Matt. 27:54). The earthquake concept demonstrates how upsetting the loss has been for you as a parent. It feels like an upheaval or shaking of the foundation of your expected life journey. What was a smooth path now has gaping sinkholes and boulders that have tumbled onto the path, making each step into the future feel uncertain and almost impassable. Your world has been shaken. You felt in control and now you may be afraid to take a step forward for fear of the unknown. Your once-smooth path now feels unreliable with broken rocks and craters surrounding you.

The darkness, the tear in the fabric of life, and the earthquake are normal reactions to loss. Identifying them as a part of the journey to grief recovery will serve as a bridge to the contentment of living again.

Sabbath

Now let's look at what follows those initial feelings. There is a Sabbath in the grieving process. The next image in the grief model springs from the orders given to the centurions (guards/soldiers) to insure that Jesus was dead after he was crucified (put to death on the cross). The action was to pierce his side to insure that Jesus was dead so they could bury him before the Sabbath began. (The Sabbath is the worship day of the week still observed by those of the Jewish faith.) When the soldiers pierced Jesus with a sword (or spear), they were surprised to find that Jesus was already dead, as we read about in John 19:34a: "Instead, one of the soldiers pierced Jesus' side with a spear. . . ."

The Sabbath in Jesus's time, as it is now, began at sundown on Friday and ended at sundown on Saturday. Devout Jews observe the Sabbath tradition today as they did two thousand years ago. No work, no driving of cars, no food preparation, and no social activities of any kind are to be done during the Sabbath. The Sabbath is a quiet time of recovery from the past week with reverence and worship as the focal point. Each human who has experienced a profound loss needs this elongated quiet time to rest and recover (physically, emotionally, and spiritually). For you, it will not be a twenty-four-hour day that you observe as a Sabbath, but it will be many days, months, and perhaps years as you recover from the death of a loved one. You will need time to be able to resume living again in a contented and joyous way. Everyone who grieves needs to rest and recover while they process the loss.

Resurrection into a New Life

The final step in the grief model is a resurrection into a new life. Again remember that you will be forever changed by the loss of your child. Like Jesus, you will be a new being when you have walked through the valley of the shadow of death and have come to a place where you have found hope and peace. The Resurrection, or raising from the dead, which was further proof that Jesus was God's Son, resulted in his countenance being changed. He had been through a horrific death. His body had lain in a tomb for three days. If we think about it in human terms, Jesus should have been "a mess." But he was not. In the resurrected life, he was transformed and some said he was actually glowing. You will not initially describe yourself as glowing when you speak of the loss of your child. However, you can move toward a life that radiates the love of God. That shining radiance is like no other. Shine on!

You can claim a new resurrected life. What will that look and feel like? Each person has a different experience. New perspective, new relationships, and new knowledge will develop from this event in your life. A new vocabulary will start to form and be used about how you feel. The use of medical terminology and the insight into how you and others mourn a loss will take form in your thinking. Take time to review your "new self." This change is not good or bad, just different. You are a new being as a result of this tiny life that started in the womb and in your life.

The Bible says God created the heaven and earth in seven days. The death and resurrection of Christ took place over three days. It will take you more than three days to mourn a significant loss. But the model still applies. Even if you are not a Christian, this model of the events presented in the Easter weekend holds true. You will feel darkness. You will feel like the foundations of your life are shaken. You will experience a tear in the fabric of your life. You will need to observe a Sabbath period to recover and, finally, you can move toward a time of joy and contentment again in your life.

Take time to look and think about your present location on the three-day journey. Are you at 3:02 on Friday afternoon just after the loss? Or are you somewhere on Saturday, the Sabbath? Are you still recovering with the shadows of sadness lessening each day? Has the earth settled back into relatively solid ground and the new routine of living life now leaves you feeling somewhat normal again, or are there still vast craters to navigate almost every day?

This model applies to all types of losses, as noted earlier (death of a parent, sibling, spouse, friend, and also to other losses like a pet, job, or financial stability). Reflecting on the model assures you of God's love for you. He did not forsake you. He did not cause your child to die, but he will be with you as you walk the three days of mourning.

CHAPTER 4

What Do You Do Now?

SPECIFIC STEPS CAN aid the healing of your wounded soul. They can bring hope and contentment to you as you move through your journey of mourning. God's model is a guide to the grief process. In the chapters to follow, the steps and concepts will be helpful to you in recovering from a miscarriage or the death of your child. These steps can ease your journey to recovery.

Concrete Steps to Coping and Recovery

1. Health care
2. Name the baby
3. Consider a funeral or memorial service
4. Expect new behaviors
5. Expect strong emotions

Step 1 – Health Care

For the mother, your first job is to seek medical care for yourself after a miscarriage or any other type of death of your child, to insure your physical health is not at risk. Be committed to taking good care of yourself. That means drinking lots of water, eating well-balanced meals, and staying on a routine for daily activities, which would include the time you get up and go to bed. Keeping a routine will help to reset the structure that has been and is disrupted when a loss has been experienced.

Follow the advice of your health care professional regarding your medical recovery. Discuss the recommendations with *all* of your family who know about the death or loss of your child. Then wisely determine the best steps for you at this time. Support from others who know about your loss will act as a gentle salve to your wound.

Romans 8:37-39 tells us, "No, in all these things we are more than conquerors through him who loved us. For I am convinced that neither death nor life, neither angels nor demons, neither present nor the future, nor any powers, neither height nor depth, nor anything else in all creation will be able to separate us from the love of God that is in Christ Jesus our Lord."

Step 2 – Name the Baby

Let's think about the next concrete step toward coping and recovery after a miscarriage. Naming the baby is important because it is a tangible reference to the loss. Perhaps if the sex of the baby was not determined when the miscarriage occurred, a non-gender-specific name may be a good option. Names like Chris, Lynn, Lee, Jade, or Taylor may be among the choices. Perhaps a name like "Baby J" honoring the month when the baby would have been born or in honor of a special person in your life, can be chosen. You would give significant consideration to names for a baby that was born at full term. You can honor this child as well with a name that means something to you. If you have experienced several miscarriages, name each baby. It is never too late to select a name for your child even if your loss happened many years ago.

Try the name by saying out loud statements like: "Baby J lived eleven weeks after conception. That was in 2010." When someone asks if you are a parent or how many children you have, you can reply, "I am the parent of three children. One lives in heaven. His name is John. He was named after his grandfather in 2010. The other two children, Susan and Tom, are in elementary school and live a crazy and fun life with their dad/mother and me." Avoid saying, "I/we had a miscarriage in 2010." The identity of your child and the ability to speak and say the name gives you control. Control is a big part of coping with loss or losses of any type.

In Isaiah 43:1, we read: "But now, this is what the Lord says – he who created you Jacob, he who formed you, Israel: "'Do not fear, for I have redeemed you; I have summoned you by name; you are mine.'" This promise is an assurance that God has called your tiny child to him and he called him or her by name.

For some parents, naming the baby makes the loss very tangible. Those parents may feel that naming the baby is an additional layer of loss. This decision is personal and should be honored. Careful consideration should be made in either case.

Step 3 – Consider a Funeral or Memorial Service

When you look at the potential your child had and review the impact he or she could have made, a funeral or memorial service is appropriate and worthy of consideration.

With the death of your child, a blood line ended that might have gone on for generations. If your child had lived through delivery, infancy, toddlerhood, childhood, pre-teen, teen, young adult, adulthood with the potential of being a mother or father of other babies, your child, tiny as it was, would have mattered and had an impact on many. Not only you, your spouse, and the lost child's siblings, but grandparents, cousins, aunts, and uncles all would have known your child. Adding to that list your child's future classmates, co-workers and friends, this precious life, though so short, is worthy of recognition. Even if it has been a long time since the miscarriage or death of your child, you can still create a celebration. You will be freer to live abundantly by acknowledging your child when you have honored his or her existence.

Simply gathering in the home, at the graveside of another relative, or at a park or having an actual service in a funeral home or church helps give the life of your child meaning. It is never too late to observe a date or have a ceremony for a loved one.

To give structure to the event, you can include prayer, singing a song or two, releasing helium-filled balloons, or reading a poem or a letter. Allow time for crying and a time to say good-bye. All of these mark, for those who mourn, a worthy recognition that this tiny little being counted. It is important to create your own celebration or moment of closure. An authentic and significant celebration for you and your family is a sacred stop on the path toward healing and an opportunity to remember this precious life. Writing a letter, lighting a candle, or just saying out loud, "I missed knowing you," opens the pathway to genuine recovery from the loss. Many families remember this date of celebration annually.

Tiny Sips

To speak the name of my beloved is like honey on my lips.
Sweet memories that could have been, I taste in tiny sips.
Your smile, your laugh are lost in my tears.
Your earthly presence is hidden from my ears.
The pain recedes, my soul is healed,
Come, Holy Spirit, be my hope and my shield.

Sharon Fox

Step 4 – Expect New Behaviors

Expect to cry. Crying is a cathartic release of emotional pain. The toxins or chemicals in the tears of those who grieve are different from the chemicals found in the tears of someone who is crying due to physical pain. Crying is actually good for you. It is appropriate and wise to cry. However, if you cry for more than a few minutes, you *must hydrate* yourself by drinking water. Crying will deplete the brain of the needed hydration levels it must have to work properly. The neuropathways will not work normally; thus thinking is confused when dehydration has occurred. *Drink water!*

You may, to your surprise and the surprise of others, find that laughing is also a physical and emotional release of the pain. Laughing that moves into crying is normal. Be in the moment when you cry or laugh. You are easing the painful pressure on your soul when you freely express your emotions. Laughing is not a betrayal of your grief. Do not feel guilty if you laugh.

Expect to experience changes in eating patterns. Your body is under heavy stress, both physically (for mothers) and emotionally. Both parents may find their diet choices shifting to excesses in "comfort foods," which often have higher calories with lower nutritional value. One or both of you may be in the other camp, eating very little. Your best hedge of protection is to return to a normal diet, which will help reset your body to "feeling normal."

If you have had a miscarriage or a stillbirth, expect to be in need of more rest. Mothers, if your miscarriage was accompanied by surgery (in some types of pregnancies), your body is recovering from anesthesia and pain management drugs and is working hard to heal the surgical assault. It is normal for the body to need additional rest to recover. If the miscarriage did not involve medical interventions, your body is still under stress. Be patient and let the physical healing unfold on its own time.

Mothers who have experienced SIDS or another kind of infant death will also need extra rest. It is part of the wounded soul's way of healing. Sleep allows the body to spend energy in the right places. Rest. It will heal your body and soul.

Fathers, to your surprise you may find yourself exhausted too after your spouse has experienced a miscarriage. Whether your child has died at birth, soon after birth or prior to birth, the sudden loss will render you fatigued with emotions as volatile as your spouse's. Naps and retiring early, which may have been very rare for you, begin to shape your desired recovery path. Keep in mind that your stress level and the additional responsibility of caring for your wife and perhaps other children requires extra energy. Your energy pool may empty faster than before. A nap is not wimping out. It is taking care of you so you can take care of others.

Expect to experience hormone-driven behavior. As a mother, your body has had a "chemical dump" that is normal during pregnancy. A divine plan for a baby to develop and for your body to supply the needed environment for the gestation (growing) process is accomplished by hormones produced in the body. When a miscarriage occurs, your body becomes confused about what to do with these chemicals. Depending on the number of weeks your baby lived after conception, the chemical oxytocin will be released. The lay term for oxytocin is "the cuddle chemical." It creates the desire to have physical contact with a baby, which is the nurturing, instinctual response to the baby's need for food and physical comfort (warmth and clean diapers). It creates the need to rock and hold the baby, which results in brain development as well as assisting in a baby's ability to reflect the emotion that it has been shown. It is critical to the baby's development, because oxytocin in the mother is almost magical in its resulting behaviors. However, when the baby has not lived to term, or is stillborn or a SIDS child, the presence of the oxytocin in the mother's body still creates the need to hold and cuddle. In post-miscarriage, stillbirth, or SIDS/infant deaths, the feeling and behaviors are called **"Empty Arms Syndrome."** It is the chemically induced desire for physical contact.

Fathers develop higher levels of oxytocin as well. The planning and desire for a pregnancy and a baby raise the male levels, which create a normal response to his child at birth. Fathers want to hold and cuddle due to elevated levels of oxytocin.

Sometimes the behaviors that result from elevated oxytocin levels become the driving force in stronger sexual behavior. The need to hold, cuddle, and express love is transferred to your spouse. Again, careful assessment of the hormonal drive and chemical behaviors is important. Talk about the strong desires and be sure you are ready for the resulting consequences of your hormone-driven behavior.

Without knowledge about the changes in chemical and hormonal levels in the body for both mother and father, the post-miscarriage, stillbirth, or infant death may take both parents to places that they did not really want to go at this time. This knowledge may prevent unexpected or untimely pregnancies. Think about what you really want now and for the future.

Empty Arms Syndrome can be experienced by both mothers and fathers and is first recognized by an achy arm sensation. This "Empty" feeling is normal. You are feeling the same thing that other mothers and fathers who have experienced a miscarriage, stillbirth, infant death, or SIDS death have felt. Don't be alarmed if this longing for something to cuddle occurs to you not only in the form of a physical ache but also in an emotional desire. It is normal and is the way the body is designed to behave. Find a way to gently ease the ache with healthy substitutes. Professionals suggest a toy like a bunny, fuzzy bear, a soft heart-shaped pillow, a quilt, or a pet that is prone to long periods of human contact as helpful and healthy cuddling objects. (A baby doll is not recommended.) Many parents tell of planning for a few minutes each day or a few weeks to sit and hold the object. This simple activity releases the stress that the absence of a child has created.

You may experience **"Shadow Grief."** Just when you thought you were coping really well, you are surprised by a significant emotional overload. That sensation is called a Shadow Grief event. It is a part of the grief process and is important to recognize and be prepared to experience. Don't think that you have regressed. Shadow Grief occurs very often unexpectedly and feels like someone snuck up behind you and poured a barrel of hot emotions on you from behind. A smell, a sudden memory, a sound of a baby crying, a conversation with someone who speaks of a child, a photo, or sonogram can trigger a Shadow Grief Event. If you are not alone when one of these events happens to you, don't be embarrassed. Just say to others "Give me a minute, I am having a Shadow Grief moment."

You will be amazed at how thoughtful people will be when you share briefly a sacred moment of mourning. Generally, that emotional assault passes quickly and your recovery is calmly achieved. In some cases, the anniversary date of the miscarriage or child death will be preceded by a few days of Shadow Grief. Again, recognize what it is and know that it will pass. Don't be disheartened. Shadow Grief Events will become less emotionally charged as time passes. If your grief lasts for more than a few days and renders you unable to function, seek professional help.

Expect to reflect on your dreams *of* and *for* your child. Your memories or unspoken dreams for your child are in tune and natural for a parent to experience. These are the hopes for health, a happy childhood, and success as an adult. The "what might have beens" have stopped with the ending of the pregnancy or the death of your child and are ground zero of the emotional loss.

Milestones of anticipated dates that would have marked key events become memory markers. They can cause high emotions or anxiety when important dates would have been observed, such as the first day of school, learning to drive, or the year of high school graduation. These are stored in the memory of the parent, not by purposeful date observances, but by the way we, as humans, are designed. No matter when your child died, those markers will likely bring sadness or at a minimum, a "pause" on or around those important dates. Don't be surprised if as these dates occur, you find yourself sad or experiencing a period of mourning. This type of emotional impact is *very* normal. Life markers will show up unexpectedly. It is the way God wired us—to anticipate and celebrate even when the celebration is only a memory of what was to have been.

Expect questions. As you recover physically, the next phase of the reconciliation of a miscarriage or infant death is to deal with the emotional aftermath. Some call it the Question Closet. It can be best described as opening a door to a closet without an overhead light. It is filled with empty hangers. The hangers represent the many questions you have about the details of how your child died. You long to place garments of useful information on the hangers, but for now there are very few tangible items to fill the empty hanger space. The questions include:

- ❏ Why me?
- ❏ Is/was this my fault?
- ❏ How could this happen?
- ❏ Is there someone to blame?
- ❏ Is there something to blame?
- ❏ Is this some sort of punishment for things I did or did not do?
- ❏ What should I do differently?
- ❏ Is there a purpose for my child's death?
- ❏ Can I trust God?

The list can go on and on. You may be accustomed to digging deep and getting answers to life's tough questions. After discussions with health care professionals, you may have some good answers, no answers at all, or more questions than you can begin to organize in your mind about your miscarriage or the death of your child. The truth is, you may never know what caused your miscarriage or the death of your child. You have experienced a devastating loss that has had a huge impact on you and your family. However, this event is not, nor should it become, the centerpiece of your life. God promises to walk with you through the valley of the shadow of death. You are to fear no evil. He did not say it (living) would be easy. He *did* promise to be with us.

Let's say that, like the cause of your child's death, you may not ever know until you reach heaven how to make sense of all of this. Decide to accept the fact that you will not know what happened, if that is the case. The one sweet thought that brings comfort to many is the concept that the purpose of the death was for your loved one to be at the gates of heaven to greet you when you die. How wonderful for your child to be standing by Jesus, God, and the Holy Spirit to welcome you into the eternal place of joy and light. Take comfort that a welcoming committee is forming at the gates of heaven as you read this book.

All of us will die. Your body will wear out. So let it be said that looking for the purpose of your child's death is not a quest worthy of your time and effort. Instead seek to appreciate the long (or short) life that you are able to share with others during your lifetime here on earth. Some people have left you in a matter of days or weeks, while others have shared time and relationships throughout your lifetime. But the true joy comes when you can hold on to God's promise that you will be comforted by the Holy Spirit as you journey through grief. Most important, you will see those you loved again as you join them in heaven. They will be fully alive and fully in harmony with God's divine plan.

Psalm 23 has been a source of comfort for many:

The Lord is my shepherd, I lack nothing.
He makes me lie down in green pastures,
He leads me beside quiet waters,
He refreshes my soul.
He guides me along the right paths for his name's sake.
Even though I walk through the darkest valley,
I will fear no evil, for you are with me;
Your rod and your staff, they comfort me.
You prepare a table before me in the presence of my enemies.
You anoint my head with oil;
My cup overflows.
Surely your goodness and love will follow me all the days of my life,
And I will dwell in the house of the Lord forever.

This psalm describes the peace and contentment that are available even in the midst of a storm as awful as the death of a child. The valley has a shadow over it. That is your sadness. God directs you to first rest by the waters. Then journey on to the table he has set before you. It has bowls of blessings and platters of joy and peace. The banquet is waiting for you. It is God's provision for you as you trust in him to bring you through your grief. Read it over and over so that it will soak into your soul and bring you contentment.

Step 5 – Expect Strong Emotions

If questions are not enough to overwhelm you, feelings of failure, disappointment, and shame can often be unrelenting shadows that follow you all day and all night. You can take another solid step toward regaining the strong emotional grounding you desire. Prepare for new emotions to impact your life.

Sadness is absolutely normal. It works like the balance of a scale that has love on one side and sadness on the other. If you love deeply, you will grieve deeply. There is not a way to "cut to the front of the line" to avoid sadness when a loved one has died. If you knew him or her for a few days, weeks, or months, this tiny miracle of life, you already know you had felt love for them. A death is not a situation to be overcome nor a problem to be solved. It is the natural response to the loss of a precious life that has ended. Your response to this loss is the way God made you and every mother and father who wanted to be or found themselves pregnant. Although this situation is very unfair, be accepting of your sadness. It is normal to suffer emotionally. Feeling sad, feeling depleted by the loss, and grieving deeply is a sign that your soul has been wounded.

You may have lots of things to be angry about. You have a right to be frustrated, distressed, disappointed, and flat-out enraged. The key again is not to let this anger control your life and poison the other really good parts of your life. Finding healthy ways to dispel the anger and to move the "flaming red" anger out of the way are important. Your lifelong joy depends on the management of anger from this event. Don't let anger brew and separate you from the lovely things of life that you already have or that await you. You did not deserve for this to happen, but you do deserve, as God's child, to feel the joy and peace that He promises to all his beloved children. Seek contentment. Joy will follow.

You may not experience anger at all. In fact, you may see that God's hand of mercy was at work and you are thankful for his loving care, which saved your child from a long journey of pain and struggle. If that is the case, rejoice in God's provision.

As a note to reflect upon for you as a parent who has experienced the death of a child, I wish to point out that prior to this loss, you were probably reasonably happy with your life. Parenting other children, a relationship with your spouse, a job, a safe place to live were things that made your life satisfying. Don't forget that those things still exist. You were happy before, and you can be happy again with the recognition that you can move through this loss. Contentment is the sweet honey of life. Count your blessings.

Resentment

Do you have a girlfriend or family member who is pregnant or has had several children without any miscarriages? That seems so unfair, especially when they seem to take for granted their ability to just decide they will get pregnant and they do. It is so easy to fall into the trap of resentment. Your struggle may have been a pregnancy after a long battle with infertility, a carefully planned for first child, or the recognition that you are pregnant again but you are unable to carry the baby to a healthy birth. Reality did not fulfill your expectation.

Resentment can take control of your thoughts and poison your joy as well as create feelings of hostility toward those who have been blessed with easy pregnancies. If you find the interaction painful, consider a frank conversation with those who may have unintentionally, or due to other circumstances, caused distress in your life. Let them know that it is the situation, not them, that has created the stress in the relationship. Ask them to be patient with you as you process your loss and in time return to a friendship/relationship that is not simmering with resentment. You don't know how much your open and honest confession of your feelings may enable others to restore relationships and rebuild friendships. Your commitment to authentic expression of your feelings will allow God to use this very sad event to glorify him in the future.

A very wise statement often quoted about resentment is: Resentment is the poison I drink in the hopes that it will kill you. Resentment does nothing to change the situation. It simply pulls you down, like an anchor, into depression.

Blame is like a huge, heavy slab of rock. You can step over it or you can pick it up and carry it around, looking for a place to lay it down. The burden is heavy! Sometimes you will have a clear location in mind for the blame to be placed. Then, after placing the "blame slab" just where you want it, you begin to quickly gather and stack layers of details like "planks of assumptions" and "bricks of discontent" upon that slab. When the construction is well underway, you may step back and realize that the "blame slab" and all the building materials rising up on top of it are blocking the way to a joy-filled life. Many parents have built elaborate blame structures that have prevented them from enjoying contentment and joy. Check your blueprints. Are you under construction?

Recognize that you or others may have placed the "blame slab" at your doorstep. Carefully, oh so carefully, see the blame for what it really is. It is highly unlikely that blame is yours unless you have taken risks such as using alcohol or drugs or having an abortion, which can impact the pregnancy. Be honest, if that is the case. Take responsibility, not blame.

Choose to accept this event. If you can't accept the loss, you may remain unhappy for the rest of your life. That is a terrible way to live. Do not accept unhappiness as your lifelong companion. It will separate you from supportive friends and family. It will push you into a corner of distrust and depression. Unhappiness is not a friend. Don't let it stay long if it shows up and rings the doorbell of your life. Acceptance of bad things and trusting that God is in control will open the way to healing and contentment.

Don't fail to choose to accept your story. No blame! Acceptance is one of the mysteries of life. Let this event create compassion for others, tenderness in self-care, respect for your mate, and honesty in your life. God is faithful in all things. Trust him to make all things good even when that seems impossible. These Bible verses can help you:

"And we know that in all things God works for the good of those who love him, who have been called according to his purposes" (Rom. 8:28).

"Because of the Lord's great love we are not consumed, for his compassions never fail. They are new every morning; great is your faithfulness" (Lam. 3:22-23).

The peace that passes all understanding is the knowledge that God loves you and he does understand your loss. His son died too.

Real or unidentified guilt holds hands with blame, resentment, and anger to form an unhealthy emotional blockade to joy. It digs deep into the mind to push peace out of the daily life experience. It makes every event, whether minor or major, a rock that will block the road to contentment. Like blame, it can be carried around as a burden that drains the energy out of living. Walk around it or step over it on your road to contentment and peace. Guilt can be and often is imagined. Don't give it life or reality. Guilt is anger turned inside.

Shame

There is a saying, "With secrets come shame." A miscarriage is *nothing* to be ashamed of! Nor is the death of your child a shame-based event. Because of the very private nature of the loss, a secret may have unintentionally been created. Due to the shortness of the pregnancy or life, and with the resulting physical issues that accompany the loss, the secret may have taken root. Friends, even close family members, may not have known about the pregnancy and thus when the miscarriage or death is discussed, they are doubly surprised about what has happened. The fear of the revelation of a miscarriage or the death of your child causes a need to remain silent about the loss for many families. This creates a thin line between honesty, timing, and privacy. It is your choice to keep the miscarriage or the death of your infant a personal secret. Perhaps you feel the secret needs to be held because it is too painful to discuss. However, be cautious about secrets and how and who keeps them. Deception may be assumed when the truth is finally revealed.

Often mothers feel the questions that are asked of them cause deep and yet unintended hurt. Questions such as, "How soon will you try again?" or "What did you do?" or "You can always get pregnant again, right?" stab the heart and wound the soul. Be prepared for the injury that words can cause. Forgive those who say such things to you. They have no idea how harmful and hurtful they are to you as you grieve.

Take the time to identify the emotions that seem to be your constant companions. Sadness, guilt, anger, resentment, bewilderment, confusion, and so many more. Name them. Say them out loud. Let yourself hear your voice as you say, "I am really _____!" As you do that, you take responsibility and control of your emotions. If you can be honest by identifying and describing what you feel, you can regain control. This is one more positive step toward healing.

The canister that holds emotions will have many other emotions within. This book only includes a few of the most common ones. Your commitment to identify your feelings, say them out loud, and write them down to create a dialogue to process every day will ease the burden you carry.

Ask yourself, "How do I feel today?" If you have or hold on to sadder feelings that seem to overtake your total being, seek professional help. Remember, you are not the only parent to have experienced a miscarriage or the death of a child. Other parents have suffered and grieved and then moved on to be happy and content. Finding joy with your spouse, your family, and friends and developing new or deeper interest in activities that make up life are concrete steps for your recovery from grief.

This loss is not to be the centerpiece of your life. Living each day in contentment is to be the centerpiece of your life. Live it fully and fruitfully, as God calls you to respond. Fruitfulness in this case is not necessarily bearing children. It is bearing the fruit of the Spirit:

"But the fruit of the Spirit is love, joy, peace, forbearance, kindness, goodness, faithfulness, gentleness, and self-control. Against such things there is no law" (Gal. 5:22-23).

"And this is my prayer: that your love may abound more and more in knowledge and depth of insight, so that you may be able to discern what is best and may be pure and blameless for the day of Christ, filled with the fruit of righteousness that comes through Jesus Christ—to the glory and praise of God" (Phil. 1:9-11).

CHAPTER 5

Where Is Hope?

THE ONE THING about hope is that it is eternal. It also comes in unexpected packages. Most of the time, not in the ones you might have anticipated, but in real honest bubbles of delight. Hope is based on expectation and thankfulness. What are you thankful for? You live in a country where you can drink clean water, the food supply is safe, and freedoms such as basic education, law and order prevail, to name just a few. Family, friends, and church support are available if you are bold enough to ask for help. Hope comes from God and dwells within us. It blooms into contentment and joy. Hold on to hope.

Romans 5:2b-5 tells us, "And we boast in the hope of the glory of God. Not only so, but we also glory in our sufferings, because we know that suffering produces perseverance; perseverance, character; and character, hope. And hope does not put us to shame, because God's love has been poured out into our hearts through the Holy Spirit, who has been given to us."

You can hope for your life to resettle into a new routine (post miscarriage or after the death of your child). You can hope for another pregnancy that will result in a child you long to nurture and love. You can hope for restoration of any broken relationships, either now or in the past. You can hope for clarity about how this event will impact the way you value life and honor those around you. You can hope, as time passes, for the sadness to recede and for acceptance of the current circumstances to be evident each day. You can hope for this loss to enable you to influence the lives of others by your example as a parent who has lost a child. Your witness of walking through this loss can bring hope to others who have experienced a miscarriage, SIDS or infant death, or stillbirth. Honor the sacred knowledge of how this loss has felt. Share, when the time comes, your journey and your claim of hope with other parents or with families who have had a loss too.

Most important, your hope is in the knowledge that you will see your child again. Claim God's promise that for those who love the Lord, they will be raised up together to live in the presence of God, Jesus, and the Holy Spirit for eternity.

Plan to be Content Again

Cross the bridge to contentment. In Cambridge, England, there is a famous wood footbridge called the Mathematical Bridge. It was constructed in 1749 with reproductions rebuilt several time since the original structure was designed by William Etheridge and assembled by James Essex. The attraction of the bridge is that it appears to the eye to be arched, yet the timbers are all straight. The angles and intersections of braces in the design create a self-supporting structure that crosses the River Cam.

Each plank and component plays an important role in the strength and stability of the structure. The four steps to contentment—cry, talk, think, and write—can be thought of as the key pieces of your bridge's structure, which will serve as the safe passage to the "bank of contentment." Neglecting to write or avoiding thinking about the loss will weaken the structure. In fact, if some piece is missing it may render your bridge so weak and shaky that passage is not possible. Each component needs equal attention in order to build a path to the new chapter in your life.

Think of it this way: Each of the four activities in the recovery structure needs to be fully functional because on the bank of contentment there is a new planting of seedlings. They are labeled happiness, joy, peace, and trust. You really want to get yourself over the river and into the radiant life and future that God has already planned for you. Get out your worker's apron, load up the tools, and start the construction of your bridge as you cry, talk, think, and write.

When you cry, set the timer for ten minutes (or some other reasonable amount of time) and let the tears flow. If you are not finished crying when the timer goes off, get up and do something that requires your mental focus. Then, if you still feel sad, which would be normal, set the timer again. Manage your tears. Not because others don't want to see you crying but because you need a physical break from crying. *You must drink water* to insure you stay hydrated. Remember, those tears have different chemical elements in them than ones you might shed from an injury. Crying is normal. Crying releases toxins and actually will make you feel better.

Talk about how you feel. Say out loud the words that actually express your feelings, anxieties, and the reality of your current situation. Talk to someone you trust who will not judge or try to manage your grief for you. Talking is the release of the pressure that builds up emotionally and damages your soul. Talk, one sentence at a time, until you can say three or four sentences all at one time about this experience. State how you feel emotionally, spiritually, and physically about your current condition. Dump it all out there. As a part of your talking points, include what you are looking forward to in the future. Articulating the future is a great source of hope.

There is great healing when you can tell your story. When you can be at peace with your story, it will no longer hold you back from living as God desires you to live. A life that is fully thankful for blessings is a life that is brimming with peace and joy. Talking about what you are thankful for may seem impossible at first, but focusing on thankfulness changes you and your circumstances. Count your blessings every day.

Think about how the miscarriage or the death of your child has and will affect your life. Ask yourself, *How do I feel about another pregnancy? Do I think in time I would want to take the risk of pregnancy again, knowing how hard this has been? How do I feel about other women who seem to just "pop out" babies without any problems at all? How will I feel if I miscarry or my next child carries the same genetic marker which could lead to death at or soon after birth? How will I feel about parenting? Do I have a spouse who will stay the course if there is another loss?* These are legitimate questions that are rarely spoken but so often are thought about in private. Write them down. Speak them out loud, not out of fear that they will come true, but out of honest processing of thoughts that are real and contribute to the sense of loss and anxiety you carry.

Control eases anxiety. Communication assists you in gaining control. Don't prolong the anxiety by avoiding the opportunity to pray and seek God's divine healing by identifying and talking to him about the concerns of your mind, heart, and soul. God can do wondrous things with the losses in your life. Allow him to heal your broken heart and restore your wounded soul. Ask him.

Think about how you can use this experience to enrich your future and your life's contribution to others. Think positively, even when you feel sad. It is *okay* and *normal* for you to be sad, but follow it with the thought that you are expecting to feel better soon. Don't give up. Joy is waiting for you. Over and over, mothers and fathers express that the loss (the miscarriage, the death of their child) was the hardest thing they had experienced, but it brought new perspective to living. Contentment and joy do return to the parents who look forward to healing by God's divine provision.

Writing or Journaling

Writing may not be your thing. Even if you don't write anything but your own signature, write a love note to your baby, using cursive. Avoid typing or printing. The emotional (right) side of the brain is connected to the logical (left) side of the brain when writing is in cursive. Using both sides of the brain will enable your emotions and thought processes to come into sync. When they are in sync, you will have the ability to experience reality from a calm perspective. You may want to write about how you feel or what plans you had for the baby's life. Tell the baby the name you selected. Say that you miss him or her so much even when you only knew them for some brief days, weeks, or months. Allow the tears to flow, the emotions to flow, and the heartache to flow onto the paper. You do not necessarily have to share with others this material that you have written by hand. Just know that the release and comfort it will bring you will reward you.

One more tip, it is often recommended that writing is the key to settling nightmares down, which may be robbing you of much needed sleep. If you are waking in the middle of the night or having difficulty going to sleep, write. As you off load the relentless images that keep you from peaceful sleep, your mind will be able to release the unresolved emotions and rest will follow. Keep a blank book and pen close by so that when you are experiencing sleep disruptions, you can journal the concerns you feel. Generally, after several recordings the disruptions become less intrusive and the nightmares decrease. If the nightmares have disturbing endings and shock you into sudden wakefulness, write in your journal a new ending. Write a creative and peaceful and happy ending where God is present and is the loving heavenly Father holding your baby in his arms.

You may want to create a memory box for your baby. When you think of your baby, you can jot a little note and put it in the box. The box may hold other tangible items, perhaps items from the hospital or the planned nursery, as well as your notes of love. If you have other children who are grieving the loss, a box for them to fill is a sweet way to honor the sibling they did not know here on earth or knew for only a brief time. A residing place for memories and thoughts gives your soul a chance to heal a bit more.

CHAPTER 6

How Do You Find Happy?

MAKE A LIST of things that make you happy. List at least ten actionable items that you can select from every day that will bring you happiness. Then select one or two each day and be intentional to do them. Be sure your list does not include drugs, risky behavior, or alcohol. Perhaps your list would include: bubble bath, music, baking cookies, smell of fresh flowers or a favorite fragrance, a memory of a sunset, looking at photos or an activity that is relaxing and soothes your soul. Foods or flavors like sugar, chocolate, cinnamon, or vanilla might be added to the list. Friends, family, or spending time in a safe and quiet place can smooth out the wrinkles of sadness. Remember "a good hair day" for mother or a task completed for dad can lift the spirit of those who mourn. Make a list and then choose a few, so you can find "your" happy. Be safe!

Happy List:

1. _Taking a walk in the woods_
2. _Riding the four wheeler_
3. _Fishing/hunting_
4. _Drawing_

5. Listening to music
6. planting flowers/vegetables
7. Swimming
8. Sitting on the front porch on a sunny day
9. Going to Lane Springs
10. Reading a good book

Expect to be happy and content again. It is God's Easter gift to each of his children. Resurrection from loss brings a radiant life. God is always faithful to comfort his children.

Marriage and Family

If you are married, the loss of a child from miscarriage, SIDS, infant death due to illness or abnormality, or stillbirth puts your marriage at risk. Seventy-five percent of the marriages who experience SIDS, stillbirth, or early infant death end in divorce. There is very little statistical information on how marriages are impacted when a miscarriage has occurred. The loss through a miscarriage, no doubt, does take a toll on a marriage. It is important for couples who have had these types of losses to be very intentional about nurturing and maintaining a solid marriage.

Other Children

If there are already other children in your family, they will grieve. They may not know what a baby sister or brother's miscarriage is all about, but certainly death, as in stillbirth, SIDS, or an infant death will create grief just like the adults around them are experiencing. They may not be old enough to understand the word *miscarriage,* but they will recognize that something has happened. They may not have the words or the adult insight to say, "I am grieving." But their behavior will show the loss they are experiencing. They may choose to mask the behavior so that they do not add to the family sadness. Make no mistake about it, children grieve.

What they will react to is the loss of a happy mother and father. Children under the age of eight will often be confused at the change of emotion in the home. Lots of crying, emotional highs and lows, and the absence of mother for medical appointments may lead them to think that they are somehow to blame for the "dis-ease" that has impacted their world. Assurance that they are *not* to blame for this sadness is critical to their emotional stability. Let them know Mommy is sad because a wonderful baby will not be a part of the family (in the case of a miscarriage). Children do understand sadness. Reassurance through affection, gentle touch, and words secures their trust in the world around them. Let love shine on them. If a child is old enough to love, they are old enough to grieve.

Grandparents

Grandparents of the baby have serious grief too. Share with them some of the tips from this book about a memory box, crying, writing, talking, and thinking so that they too can recover from the loss.

Family members may be eager to blame or to try to control your reaction to the loss. Breathe deeply and set good boundaries so that you can protect yourself as you grieve. Good boundaries means stating clearly to others that you honor their input; however, this experience has been the worst event in your life which will require time to heal. Tell them you are experiencing new and strong emotions about this loss, as they are. Ask them to filter their opinions through love and you will do the same.

CHAPTER 7

Intimacy after Miscarriage, SIDS/ Infant Death, or Stillbirth

THE NEXT SECTION addresses the most personal aspect of marriage—sex. This book would not be complete without addressing the topic of sex and the different perspectives that compose the fabric of the marriage. Sex can be a very difficult topic to discuss. It has the potential to create or break bonds that are based on trust and tenderness. When sex is discussed, be honest with your mate. This is another critical step in recovery that needs special attention.

Several classic male and female perspectives on sex are presented below. Your experience may be exactly like one of these or nowhere close, but knowing that the thought processes of males and females may be different is very important. Use these scenarios for perspective as you discuss sex with your spouse.

Male:

Scenario#1

I am John. I am scared to even talk, much less suggest that we have sex. I am afraid that she is not ready or that she will be angry that the loss of the baby was somehow my fault biologically. I worry that if we have sex, she could either not enjoy it like she did before the loss/death or she will blame me for getting her pregnant in the first place. I am so torn up, somewhat impatient, and confused about the mixed signals I am getting and I am very frustrated.

Scenario #2

I am Jack. I love my wife deeply. I believe that for me the expression of my love to my wife is the most pure when we have sex. I want to comfort her, to please her, and to let her know that I love her so very much. I want her to know that I am with her through this really difficult physical and emotional time. Sex seems like the right thing for us to share how deeply we care about each other. I feel the loss deeply too. I want her comfort as well to help me deal with the loss.

Scenario #3 (Infant death specific)

I am Will. Our baby died at birth (or soon after birth from SIDS). I am devastated. I need the comfort of my wife that comes only in the form of love or sex to me. I feel I deserve the same consideration that she is asking for. My wife's needs seem to be all about her, not me. I need to be comforted and sex is one of the ways for the feeling of love to be conveyed to me.

Scenario #4

I am Rob. My wife and I have had a miscarriage. We both were shocked by the suddenness of this loss. I had such dreams for this baby. I was crazy about the idea of being a dad. Now I am so scared that if we get pregnant again this could happen again. It makes my heart hurt when I think about it. And that leads me back to how this baby came to be. We had sex. Am I nuts to feel guilty, sad, angry, scared, and confused about our future family? What do I do about sex?

Female:

Scenario #1

I am Jane. I love my husband, but the thought of sex brings me to tears. I don't have real clear emotions behind the tears except to say that my body is still hormonal, my mind is jumbled with thoughts of disappointment and that this may have been my fault. Or sometimes I feel that I deserve this somehow. My husband seems to want sex and right now the idea is in no way appealing to me. I thought I had to only cope with the loss of our baby, but I now realize I have to cope with my husband and his needs and perhaps the health of our marriage as well. This is so much more complicated than I expected it to be.

Scenario #2 (Infant death/SIDS specific)

I am Stephanie. Our child died of SIDS. We had adjusted to being parents. The routine of work schedules and child care was running smoothly. Suddenly our baby boy is dead. My husband is depressed, I think. He wanted a son so badly. I am longing, aching for the intimacy that sex brings. He says his grief feels like a part of him died so he is unable to be the husband he wants to be right now. Well, that feeling of low energy applies to me as well. We have sex occasionally, but it is not meeting my needs for intimacy and cuddling. I long for him, but he is so distant. I think he is afraid that I will get pregnant again and that another child will die too.

Scenario #3

I am Ann. My husband loves me. I am sure of that, but right now sex seems to be an underlying area of stress between us. I don't want to have sex right now. I feel I need affection and physical touch, but I am afraid that sex will result in pregnancy again. If I lose another baby, I don't know if I could take the emotional and physical loss right now. I don't think I have the energy to even discuss this with him, but I know he deserves to at least have the topic addressed. I also know he is grieving for this baby too. He was as excited about Baby J as I was. We need each other, but it feels like there is a distance between us.

Scenario #4 (Miscarriage specific)

I am Ellen. Here is how I think about this: I am married. My spouse and I had sex, I conceived, pregnancy was confirmed, I had a miscarriage, and now my heart is broken. I know if I backtrack this heartache, it began with sex. I also know it is somewhat illogical to think that to avoid heartache in the future, I should stop having sex. I don't know if I want to have sex, if I am afraid of sex, or if I can process or separate the connection of sex from the heartache of the miscarriage. I know that miscarriages are sometimes not singular occurrences. When I get pregnant again, there are no guarantees that a miscarriage will not occur again. There is documentation that some women have had three, four, or more miscarriages initially or throughout the childbearing years. Can I face that? I need to figure this out.

Scenario #5 (Miscarriage specific)

I am Trisha. I am newly married. Timing for a baby was not really ideal, however, we were excited to welcome a baby this early in our marriage. A friend thinks I dodged a bullet when the miscarriage occurred because we had planned to have a few years as "just a couple" before or if we started a family. Sex has been a foundational element of our relationship. Now it feels like a risk every time we make love. Was the miscarriage a blessing or a marriage breaker? I am heartbroken over all of this. How strange to have such mixed emotions.

Reflection

Your thoughts and your spouse's thoughts are not wrong if you disagree. They are different. Take the time to respect the feelings of one another without judgment.

Even when you have the lowest level of energy and determination in your emotional pool, summon the courage to talk about sex and any other issues that are creating friction in the relationship. Finances, family relationships, and expectations of one another are just a few of the subjects that can create detrimental marriage concerns. Your marriage, peace of mind, the future for the two of you, the future of your other children (should there be siblings of this baby) demand honesty. A commitment to keep topics open for frank and gentle discussion can create common ground, no matter what the contention may be. Patience and love will flourish if you allow them to be brought into the openness of a discussion. God has a canopy of love that can cover all hurts.

CHAPTER 8

What Should You Say to Someone Who Is Grieving?

THIS BOOK HAS addressed the opportunities to share your experience with others who have experienced a loss like yours. There will certainly be situations where the loss is not like yours but you will understand the emotional burden carried by others. If you find yourself in a situation where condolences need to be expressed, here is what to say.

1. Say their name. (A name creates a bond between you and the griever. If you don't know their name, say your name instead.)
2. State the data about the loss. In one sentence, acknowledge your understanding of the loss (death of child, husband, parent, or miscarriage or divorce, etc.)
3. Say you are sincerely sorry for their loss.
4. Tell them you will pray for them.

Then don't say anything more.

The conversation might sound like this:

"John, I understand your mother, Jane, died (after surgery). I am so sorry. Please know I will be praying for you and your family."

Or

"Anne, I understand you had a miscarriage recently. I am so sorry for your loss. I will be praying for you."

Or

"Mike and Sara, I was told your son Jason has died (after his battle with cancer). I am so sorry for your loss. I will be praying for you both."

Those four items (name, data about the loss, expression of sincere sorrow for their loss, and prayer) express your compassion while respecting the boundaries of those who are in grief.

If it is in the early days and weeks after the loss, they may be unable to say more than a word or two. Don't tax them by asking questions at this time or seeking more information about the death. In a few weeks, call or contact them and ask them to tell you how they are feeling. Invite conversation with gentle open-ended questions such as "Tell me," or "Explain to me" or "Help me understand how …" If you ask, "Are you okay?" they are likely to lie to you and say "I am fine" when they are not fine.

Don't say, "God needed another angel" or "It was their time" or "Your loved one is in a better place." Those types of statements often inflict more wounds into the soul, causing anger and a deeper sense of loss.

Less is more when expressing condolences.

CHAPTER 9

Holding on to Hope

JEREMIAH 29:11-14 TELLS us, "For I know the plans I have for you," declares the Lord, "plans to prosper you and not to harm you, plans to give you hope and a future. Then you will call on me and come and pray to me, and I will listen to you. You will seek me and find me when you seek me with all your heart. I will be found by you," declares the Lord, "and will bring you back from captivity."

Bad and unexpected things happen to people. Illnesses strike, jobs are lost, accidents occur, families break apart, tiny babies are miscarried or die at or soon after birth. There is no perfect life free of disappointments and heartache. You and your family have experienced a unique and significant loss. Hope and a future, however veiled they are today, are waiting for you.

The passage from the Sermon on the Mount, found in Matthew 5:4, promises, "Blessed are those who mourn, for they will be comforted," and reminds you that you have been given a clear promise of comfort when you seek it. You will have hope and a future that is filled with God's love for you and for your baby. The sweet comfort is that God mourns along with you the death of your child here on earth, but He also celebrates the arrival of your child to live through eternity in heaven with him. Your child is living free of heartache, skinned knees, and bug bites in the presence of the heavenly Father and his Son Jesus Christ.

Someday you will pause, perhaps for just a moment, and think about the landscape of your soul. You will note the locations of deep bruises and blemishes that have healed.

Scars, both large and small, will still be visible. They will be no longer painful or tender to the touch of memories. When you recall what happened, you can speak of it without fresh emotional pain. Those scars are reminders of your life and the events that have comprised your life's journey. Remarkable healing due to the loving comfort of God will be evident. You will see the tiny scar just off center that reminds you that a very special loss occurred there, the miscarriage or the death of your child. As you recall that event, remember also this Bible verse: "Trust the Lord with all your heart and lean not on your own understanding; in all your ways submit to him, and he will make your paths straight" (Prov. 3:5-6).

You have had a unique path. Upon reflection, you can see clearly God's provision and loving guidance during those very dark days when nothing made sense. Now, somehow, you can see that the loss made you more compassionate and more aware of God's love and his tenderness, which have formed you into the person you are today. You are God's child and he loves you!

Press on. God has got you by the hand.

CHAPTER 10

The Bed

FOR THE PARENT of a miscarried child, a stillborn baby, a SIDS death or any other form of infant death, the loss and grief are profound. It is not that these parents and families are somehow needier. These families have experienced the sudden and intimate loss of their child, which is complex in its nature and brings with it deep grief. Not only has their child died, but the loss of the dream of what their child was to become has died too. There is no memory bank upon which to reflect. The impact on the mind and body causes the soul to scream: "This is so unfair! This is so wrong!" A child has died without the chance to live.

"Death is death" is an often-stated opinion that equates all types of death and loss as the same. The phrase seems to use a one-size-fits-all measuring cup of compassion and understanding. For those who have experienced the loss of a parent in late adulthood, the death is within what can be described as the "rhythm of life." When a child dies, the rhythm of life has been shockingly reversed. Parents do not expect to experience the death of their child.

Perhaps this story will help illustrate this journey of loss.

You have had the worst day of your life. Your child died today. You are still in shock and you don't understand what has happened. You are bone tired from the physical and emotional stress of the death. What you long for is a good night's sleep so that tomorrow things will be better and perhaps almost feel normal.

You find yourself walking with a small group of people who have also experienced today the death of someone they loved. All of you approach a doorway at the end of a hallway that is marked, Entrance into the Rest of Your Life. What you were seeking was your safe, comfortable bed, the one that you know so well. It has a mattress, just the right amount of comfortable covers and pillows to insure that you can sleep through the night and be restored for tomorrow. As you peer into the room expecting to see your bed, you are shocked to find nothing is the same. You see many types of beds already occupied with other sleepers and a few empty ones of various sizes. Your bed is missing. Things are nothing like they were before.

You notice a clipboard with the following note hanging by the door. "Your bed has been removed. It was taken to a shredder and totally destroyed and dumped into a landfill. You will never see or experience sleeping in that bed again. Here is your new bed assignment."

"Each person must enter the room, climb into a new bed, and fall asleep before the next one can go in," you read.

The first person in your group has experienced the death of a parent. He has a new bed, for his old comfortable place to sleep is gone too. He has a bed very similar in size to his old bed. It has about the same number of pillows and blankets as the one he had before. "Different, to be sure, but in many ways the same," he explains. He gets into the bed, pulls the covers up, and after a few minutes, slips into sleep.

The second person has been assigned a twin bed. Her husband died only hours ago. This bed is far narrower than the one she had before, she tells you. The blanket on her bed is heavy and thick and almost impossible to lift and slide under. The pillow is missing, but she positions herself in a way to accommodate the missing pillow and soon she is asleep too.

You are next. You are assigned a bed that is best described as an army cot. There are two X-shaped wooden frames attached to long wooden rods running the length of the cot. A piece of rough canvas is stretched over the four corners. There is no mattress, no blanket, no sheet, no pillow on your cot. You are expected to rest and recover from this horrific event on a "camp bed"!

As you carefully sit down on the side of the cot, you wonder about the mattresses, blankets, pillows, and sheets that many of the other people have on their beds. Where is your stuff? How can you rest on this stark and coverless platform? How can you make sense of the variety of beds and comfort items that some have and some, like you right now, do not have? You close your eyes to shut out the blinding hurt of the death of your child. You try to relax by breathing deeply.

With each breath you slowly realize that there is meaning to the strange bedding arrangements around you. The mattress represents the security that comes from the expectation of a normal life. The things that are normally anticipated to be reliable in life are the foundations of restful sleep. The blanket represents memories of the loved one.

For a person who has experienced the death of a parent or spouse, the covers are thick and heavy due to the years spent together building those memories. The pillow is the support of family and friends, which nestles the head and is filled with expressions of concern. The sheet is the buffer that spreads gently out to provide a shield from bad things in life. You have none of these right now. Your child died. There are no memories. There is little or no support from others, as they may not have even known you were pregnant (if your loss was a miscarriage). Your family may not have known your child at all (in the case of stillborn birth, SIDS, or other forms of infant death). Your child died too soon to have created deep emotional bonds with family and friends or to have filled a pool of meaningful memories for you to visit in the midst of this loss. Alone, un-buffered from the harshness of this loss, your tiny cot is without any comforting surfaces. For now, it feels like this will always be your painful new bed.

Others in the room who were already in bed and who you thought were asleep when you arrived, whisper to you in the night. "You can regain peace. You can feel God's divine love in the midst of this loss. You can ask the one true Source for comfort and contentment. You can survive this loss. With God's provision, you can be happy again."

But for a time you think, as you toss around on your cot, that such whispers are empty. You believe you will have to survive in this harsh bed of loss for the rest of your life, unless . . . What was that about the one true Source of comfort and contentment? Can I ask God through the Holy Spirit to ease my heartache? Can I ask for my bed to be transformed into a place of comfort and rest for me? I need the sure foundation of his faithfulness under me. I need a blanket of peace, a pillow of hope, and a sheet of contentment to shelter me from the pain I feel now. Can I get all of these?

The answer "Yes" burns in your mind.

I can receive grace and contentment as it flows from God into my wounded soul. I can be resurrected to peace, happiness, and joy. But how does that happen? I need to *ask*: "Ask and it will be given to you; seek and you will find; knock and the door will be opened to you. For everyone who asks receives; the one who seeks finds; and to the one who knocks, the door will be opened" (Matt. 7:7-8).

But what about those people at the end of the room still sleeping on cots without covers? Most of them appear to have been there for a while and yet they still do not have a blanket or pillow. Did they fail to seek and ask God to lift their burden of loss? Perhaps they do not want to ask for God's provision of soul-healing and life-regenerating love because they believe that the death of a child was a life sentence of sadness.

You think clearly for the first time since your child died. "I don't want to stay this way and be like them," you say to yourself. "They seem damaged, desolate, and cold." You want the comfort that comes from faith in God.

You decide to ask for the Lord's smooth, warm quilt, not made of earthly threads but made of hope layered upon peace, layered upon contentment. You want that blanket to be bound around the edges with gentleness and mercy. You long to wrap yourself in the thick garment of love that is provided by the Holy Spirit, the Holy Comforter. You claim God's promise to hold you close, knowing he cares about your heartache of loss. You ask God to remake your bed with fresh linens of his making. You know, with confidence, that his love will be with you throughout the long night of grief recovery.

Look, there, all you need is folded and waiting for you.

> But now, this is what the Lords says—
> he who created you, Jacob,
> he who formed you, Israel:
> Do not fear, for I have redeemed you;
> I have summoned you by name;
> you are mine.
> When you pass through the waters, I will be with you;
> and when you pass through the rivers, they will not sweep over you.
> When you walk through the fire, you will not be burned; the flames will not set you ablaze.
> For I am the Lord your God, the Holy One of Israel, your Savior. (Isa. 43:1-3a)

Rest in the comfort of the Savior.

About the Author

—⁂—

SHARON FOX HAS been active in Christian Grief Recovery Ministry for almost twenty years. She is co-founder of the nonprofit Brave Penny, which serves those who have had non-traditional losses of children which would include the choice of gifting a child through adoption to another family, miscarriage, SIDS/Infant death and Stillbirth. Sharon is the author of *Reframing Adoption* published in 2014 (and the Spanish version, *Replantear la Adopcion*), which is dedicated to birthparent grief recovery. The biological or birthmother/father makes a brave decision to choose not only life for their child by avoiding abortion, but to gift their child, when possible, in an open adoption to another family. The grief of choosing adoption for a child has historically been caused by shame and condemnation originating in our culture. *Reframing Adoption* reflects a fresh look at recognition of the birth family and sharing many of the same concepts on grief recovery.

Sharon is a Certified Grief Facilitator, author, teacher, and speaker. Sharon and her husband, Jim, live in Frisco, Texas.

Sharon@BravePenny.com
www.BravePenny.com

About Brave Penny Nonprofit

Brave Penny supports, through education and publications, birthmothers, birthfathers, and their families, who have chosen adoption for their child, parents who have experienced miscarriages, parents who struggle with infertility, parents who have experienced SIDS or stillbirths, and parents who have experienced the death of their adult child.

Visit the web site for other articles on grief recovery.

Your contribution to the nonprofit enables Brave Penny to provide books to pregnancy centers and mothers or families who seek a Christian-based presentation of the grief recovery journey.

Contact Information

To order additional copies of this book, please visit
www.redemption-press.com.
Also available on Amazon.com and BarnesandNoble.com
Or by calling toll free 1-844-2REDEEM.